"When I Was in Prison…
…You Visited Me"

by
Ronald "Scotty" Bourne

First printing 2008
Follow Me Communications, Inc.

© Copyright 2008, All Rights Reserved
ISBN# 978-0-9630569-0-0

2

Dedicated to the loving memory of
Reverend John "Jack" Duggan, S.J.
A special friend and spiritual father

"When I was in prison… you visited me."
Matthew 25

Preface

I can remember vividly one summer evening in Hollywood, California leaving an office on Sunset Boulevard after a Charismatic prayer meeting. A poster on the stairwell wall advertised for volunteers to get involved in a prison ministry outreach. Thinking to myself, I made the following mental comment to the Lord. "I will do anything for you Lord, but one thing I will not do is go into any prison." Why I made that comment, I don't know, but somewhere deep inside of me was a real and tremendous fear of doing such a thing. But God is good! He took my fear and turned it into a blessing.

In 1975, I volunteered as a Chaplain with the Los Angeles Archdiocese Religious Education Department in two separate juvenile detention facilities, Camps Scott and Scudder. I moved to Orange County in 1981 and continued to minister in the Orange County Juvenile and Adult facilities as well as become involved with Kairos Prison Ministry in the Federal facility at Terminal Island. I relocated north to Bakersfield in 2004, to Kern County, considered by some to be the prison capital of California, and I am presently working fulltime as a Deacon in the Church of St. Francis of Assisi. My ministry duties have led me into the following local facilities: Mesa Verde

Prison, a privately run adult prison; Kern County Juvenile Hall; Pathways, a Kern County teenage drug rehab facility; New Crossroads Juvenile Detention Camp, and trips to the nearby Tehachapi and Lerdo adult prisons. The time I've spent ministering in all these facilities has been the most spiritually fulfilling period of my life. You might say I grew up and matured as a Christian while serving the inmates. It was in my daily quest for God and seeking His will that I found Jesus among them, and very much alive in them. Our Lord used these wonderful people to show and teach me His faithfulness and love. Therefore, it would be unfair of me not to mention that I received so much more from the ministry than I ever gave.

The following stories are but a few of the many graces that I was fortunate to encounter while serving in some of these places. I pray that they will convey the Gospel truth to all who read them:

"When I was in prison... you visited me." Matthew 25

Contents:

	Preface	page	5
Chapter 1	*"My First Visit to Prison"*	page	11
Chapter 2	*"Judges 20"*	page	21
Chapter 3	*"A Letter for James"*	page	31
Chapter 4	*"Catholic or Christian?"*	page	39
Chapter 5	*"The Mouse and the Gospel"*	page	47
Chapter 6	*"A Rosary for Robert"*	page	55
Chapter 7	*"Pablo's Lucky Medal"*	page	63
Chapter 8	*"The Bandit Story"*	page	73
Chapter 9	*"A Decision for Carlos"*	page	81
Chapter 10	*"A Prayer for Crazy"*	page	93
Chapter 11	*"A Benedictine Behind Bars"*	page	103
Chapter 12	*"Edward and the Brothers"*	page	111
Chapter 13	*"Christmas Bandit"*	page	117

CHAPTER 1

MY FIRST VISIT TO PRISON

"If you please, Lord, send someone else!"
"It is I who will assist you in speaking and will teach you what you are to say."

Exodus 4:10,12,13

Chapter 1

My First Visit to Prison

I vividly remember the first time I drove out to the detention camp for a solo visit. My heart was pounding with fear and I nervously argued with myself about turning around and going home. What business did I have visiting youngsters in detention camp and how did I manage to get myself into this predicament? Those thoughts kept running through my mind as I drove the winding, country road to camp. Admittedly I had made a couple of visits to the camp prior to this, but they had been with two ladies from the local Legion of Mary. The ladies had talked me into accompanying them because they thought they needed a male escort and randomly picked me. Why me? Well, according to the ladies, I looked like a nice young man, plus I had foolishly told them that I had nothing special to do one Saturday morning after Mass.

During those first couple of visits, I quietly stood back and silently observed as the ladies handed out Rosaries and talked and prayed with the boys. While observing what was going on, I decided that this "prison ministry thing" was definitely not for me. In the prison parking lot I kept telling the two ladies that they should find someone else; another male, to accompany them. They politely listened to all my fantastic excuses such as:

"I have nothing in common with the kids in camp; they are mostly Mexican-American and Black; therefore, it would be hard for us to relate."

"Because of my Scottish upbringing and accent, if I did try to talk and communicate with them, they would never understand me anyway."

Now through a series of strange circumstances, I found myself alone in a small room filled with about thirty tough-looking teenagers, all staring at me. They sat anxiously and waited for me to say something. Although slightly panicking inside, I calmly introduced myself and mentioned that this one-hour period would be devoted to a prayer service. I nervously made the Sign of the Cross and prayed an informal opening prayer which lasted about 20 seconds, and then my mind went completely blank. I could detect the nervous perspiration beginning to build as I frantically searched for what to do next. To my utter amazement I heard myself asking the following, "Does anyone have any questions?"

A young, tough-looking Hispanic boy sitting in the back of the room quickly raised his hand. "Some guys in here call themselves Christians, but I knew them 'on the outs' (outside prison) and they weren't Christian. Do you think it's right for them to become Christians while in prison?"

Somewhat relieved at having something to say, I answered his question. "Some people who may not have been following the Lord on the outside may very well take a good, hard look at their lives when they find themselves in a place like this. Maybe it's while here they realize that their life is not going the way they would like it; and so, determined to make a change, they decide to follow Jesus. People who follow Jesus are called Christians. It doesn't make any difference where you are when you decide to follow Him. Prison is as good a place as any and there is nothing wrong in making a decision like that while in here."

Another young man near the front shot his hand up. "Some guys in here say that they have Jesus in their heart. Do you believe that?" he asked.

"Yes," I answered. "Not only do I believe it but I also have Jesus in my heart.

"How does Jesus get into your heart?" asked another of the boys.

"Well there are many ways," I began. "One way is to invite Him…"

Before I could finish, another kid called out, "How do you do that?"

"Do what?" I responded.

"How do you invite Jesus into your heart?"

"You can do that by saying a prayer…"

"Do you know that prayer?" he eagerly interrupted.

"Why, yes!" I responded, quite surprised at his eagerness.

A young, serious-looking Hispanic boy in the back of the room stood up and asked, "Would you say that prayer before you leave?"

I nodded my head, thought for a minute, and then cautioned the boys. "I can lead you all in a prayer asking Jesus into your heart, but you have to be sincere and really mean the words. God knows your heart and He can tell if you are sincere or not. You can't con God. Do you all understand what I'm saying?"

They all nodded their heads and clearly indicated that they understood.

It seemed like I had just finished answering a couple more questions when the Duty Counselor opened the door and called out to me, "You have five minutes left."

Panicking, I checked my watch - and sure enough an hour had almost slipped by. Looking at the boys, I commented, "No more questions. Let's pray."

A young man immediately shot his hand up and said, "Don't forget the prayer you promised."

"What prayer?" I responded.

"The prayer that invites Jesus into your heart."

"OK," I replied, "Remember what I said earlier, you have to be sincere. I will lead you in a prayer; just repeat the words after me." I surveyed the eager faces of the young men as they sat in their chairs waiting for me to begin the prayer.

"Dear Jesus," I began and they all responded by repeating the words. As I continued with the prayer, "Lord, I invite you into my heart and into my life," one of the young men sitting in the front row got off his chair and knelt on the concrete floor. The act of this young man kneeling in front of me, obviously sincere in his prayer, caused my heart to jump and lodge in my throat. With great difficulty and emotion I continued the prayer, and as I did so other young men unabashedly followed the example of the first. By the time we had finished the prayer inviting Jesus into our lives and hearts, most of these tough young men were on their knees.

The impact of those young boys giving their lives over to Jesus was so tremendous that I couldn't quite take it all in. I was in semi-shock.

The Duty Counselor opened the door and in about five seconds flat had all the young men lined up and marched out of the room, leaving me all alone. Silently and reflectively I made my way to the parking lot. It was only when I reached my car that the full impact of what took place really hit me. I openly cried like a baby when I realized that for weeks I had been telling God that this prison thing was not for me, and in His gentle way He was showing me that this is where He wanted me to be. So it was fitting that in that same prison parking lot, I willingly said "yes" to God. "Yes!" if He wanted me to visit the young men every week in prison for the rest of my life. My comment to God was, "If you want me to spend the rest of my lifetime going into prison and only one person gets on their knees and invites You into his life, then my visits will not be in vain."

That beautiful Saturday morning marked the beginning of a very rewarding prison ministry.

CHAPTER 2

JUDGES 20

"I command you be firm and steadfast. Do not swerve either to the left or to the right... Do not fear or be dismayed for the Lord your God is with you wherever you go."

Joshua 1: 9

Chapter 2

Judges 20

Scripture, when it becomes a "lived" experience, can have a life-changing effect in our lives. I found this out while studying the Old Testament. In the Book of Judges, Chapter 20, the four hundred thousand strong Israelite Army gathered to fight against the men of the tribe of Benjamin. The Benjaminites had a much smaller army and opposed their brother Israelis who wanted to right a wrong. The large Israelite force (the good guys) consulted the Lord and asked who should go into battle first. The Lord replied, "Judah shall go first."

Next day, as the Israelites drew up in battle formation outside the Benjamin city of Gilbeah, the smaller force of Benjaminites (the bad guys) came out and killed twenty-two thousand men of Israel. The Israelites went before the Lord and wept until the evening. "Shall I again engage my brother Benjamin in battle?" they asked the Lord.

The Lord replied that they should. The Israelite soldiers took heart, and for the second time took up battle formation against the Benjaminites. Once again the Benjaminites came out of the city of Gilbeah, and this time killed eighteen thousand Israelite soldiers. The entire Israelite army went up to Bethel, where they again wept. They remained fasting before the Lord until evening and offered holocausts and peace offerings. Again they consulted the Lord and asked, "Shall I go out again to battle with Benjamin, my brother, or shall I desist?"

The Lord answered, "Attack! For tomorrow I will deliver him into your power."

The next day, for the third time, the Israelite Army engaged the Benjaminites in battle and was victorious.

They defeated the Benjaminites and almost wiped out the whole tribe. Only a few hundred men from the Benjamin tribe survived.

What does that incident from Judges 20 tell us?

I know that when I pondered this reading and applied it to my own life, it radically changed my spiritual walk. You will notice that not once did the Israelites doubt God's word. After their first defeat, their question to the Lord was, "Shall I again engage my brother Benjamin in battle?" And the Lord answered that they should. Then, after their second defeat, still not doubting the Lord's initial word, they asked if they should continue to fight. Again the Lord told them to attack.

Their communication with the Lord was so clear that they never once doubted God's instructions to them. Regardless of the defeats that were inflicted upon them, the Israelites only continued to ask the Lord to confirm His original word to them, and questioned if He still wanted them to act on it. Not one of the Israelites mentioned that they wanted to leave the battle, or join the opposing force that seemed to be enjoying victory after victory.

Speaking for myself, if I were a member of that Israelite Army back then, I would probably have been the first one to question the leadership and God's initial word after we suffered the first defeat. Then after the second defeat, I would have loudly voiced my opinion that this was certainly a confirmation of the fact that we were not in God's will. Suffering two successive defeats would give anyone a legitimate and sound reason for questioning if they were in God's will. After all, the Israelite Army was supposed to be "the good guys." They consulted the Lord in prayer for direction before doing anything. But the amazing thing was that they never doubted or questioned the Lord's word and never allowed their feelings or the situation that confronted them to dictate otherwise to them. Regardless of their defeats, they did not allow circumstances or pain to sway them from believing God.

There was a time in the past when I prayed and believed that the Lord had spoken very clearly to me and given me direction. I would step out in faith, after confirming the word, and sometimes fall flat on my face. This would cause me great soul searching, as I would always ended up somewhat confused. Did God speak to me or did I just think He spoke to me? Usually, whenever I encountered any kind of strong resistance, I took that as a sign of God saying, "Stop!"

Believing that the Lord wants to establish clear communication with all of His people and knowing that He does not wish His people to be confused or misdirected, I decided to apply the principles of Judges 20 in my own life.

At one particular time I believed the Lord was asking me to do more for the young men in the juvenile detention camp. After discussing my thoughts with the Religious Sisters of the L.A. Archdiocese Religious Education Office, I was strongly encouraged by them to begin a weekly Catholic Bible study. This to me was a confirmation and I eagerly began to start organizing the program. But things did not go too well at first and I ran into a lot of resistance from one of the senior probation officers. He, a professed Christian, strongly believed that Catholic teaching was in error, and would always find a "legitimate" excuse for not allowing the young men to meet with me for Bible study. Looking at and assessing the situation, I began to wonder if the Lord was closing the door for me in this particular ministry outreach. In my prayer I asked the Lord if He wanted me to continue going the extra night each week to the detention camp, or to stop. Judges 20 would always come to mind, and I searched that chapter for an answer. The Lord's first words to the Israelites seemed to be the answer that witnessed deep inside of me - "Judah shall go first."

Although I listened real hard during prayer, I never heard the Lord saying, "Stop", so I continued. Remembering that Judah means "praise," I praised God during the long drive to the detention facility. For the next few months I spent the hour sitting alone each week in an empty TV room. I patiently waited for that particular camp counselor to change his mind or be moved to another camp. Every evening as I drove back home after a fruitless visit, I felt as if I were coming back from the battlefield after having been totally defeated. And every week I would repeat my painful cry, "Are you sure Lord you want me to continue?"

Then one Thanksgiving evening, on the night of my weekly visit, I was surprised to find out that there was no other scheduled camp activity. The camp counselor who opposed me was somewhat shocked to see me turn up.

"This is Thanksgiving!" he exclaimed, "All the other religious services have taken the week off. You don't have to be here."

But when I told him that this was exactly the place where I wanted to spend my Thanksgiving, a different attitude came over him. Hastily he arranged for the gymnasium to be opened up. Then he had every young man in the detention facility line up and march over to the gym. That evening, the same counselor who for the past few months had denied me access to the Catholic youth, introduced me to the whole camp and invited me to conduct a Thanksgiving service for everyone.

After the service, the counselor privately spoke to me, apologizing for his previous behavior. "I didn't know you Catholics believed like that. Everything you mentioned in the service I strongly said 'Amen' to."

Every week thereafter, he went out of his way to assist me in making sure that my Bible study took priority over anything else that happened to be going on at the camp. Not only did he ensure that all Catholic youth attend my Bible study, but he also encouraged the non-Catholic youth to attend. The principles of Judges 20 finally bore fruit, and through it all, the Lord taught me a very valuable lesson.

CHAPTER 3

A

LETTER

FOR JAMES

"humbly welcome the word that has taken

root in you, with its power to save you.

Act on this word.

If all you do is listen to it,

you are deceiving yourselves."

James 1: 21-22

Chapter 3

A Letter for James

It is amazing how the Lord can speak to you through an incident and how that one incident can change your whole focus on ministry. For me, I can clearly look back through the years and point to one young man who was instrumental in doing just that for me. His name was James. He was a young, muscular, tough-looking Hispanic, classified as a "Gang Leader" in his Los

Angeles County Juvenile Detention file. You didn't have to read his file to know that he was a troublemaker; it was clearly evident by the way he intimidated and bullied the other young inmates at the detention camp.

Over a period of months, he became a thorn in my side as he frequently paid visits to our Bible study. He would disrupt the evening either by walking out and taking half the group with him or by silencing any of the boys from sharing and reading the Scriptures out loud. He did this by giving them a mean look or a threatening hand gesture. Clearly the others feared him. I didn't know how to handle James and this kind of behavior, so I always let him walk out with the assurance that he was welcome back again anytime. Camp counselors and other kids advised me to bar him from any of my group activities or services. I must say - that suggestion did seem like a great idea, and I almost got around to doing it one night when James tried to keep a non-Catholic boy from attending the Bible study.

Ironically, James was baptized Catholic as a baby but never set foot in a church after that. He identified himself with the Church but never openly practiced what it taught. It got to the point that other kids who were serious about studying the Scriptures would wait to see if James was going or not before they would commit themselves to the Bible study each week. From a dozen or so kids who originally began the group, we slowly dwindled down to two or three faithful.

Then one evening when I visited the camp for my one-to-one counseling (the authorities only allowed me one hour per week to do this and usually I had a list of four to eight boys who wished to see me in that time frame). I arrived at the front office to sign in and James was standing near the Duty Counselor's desk. He looked a little subdued as he watched the Counselor busy himself with papers at his desk.

Looking up at me, the Counselor laughed and remarked, "Here comes Scotty! Maybe he can help."

Glancing at the Officer I asked, "What's up?"

The Officer made his way over to me and sarcastically stated, "James wants to write a letter to his mother."

"How does that concern me?" I asked.

Turning to look at James, the Officer, obviously enjoying the moment, placed his face close to James and sneered in a loud voice, "James can't write and he wants me to write it. Well, I'm too busy!"

Immediately, my own thoughts went something like, "No way am I going to take time to write a letter, especially for James. They give me one hour and I want to spend it with kids who really need me and want to see me." A thousand not just "good" but "excellent" reasons for not wanting to get involved with James had little trouble flashing through my mind. But when I completely observed the situation and saw for the first time a dejected-looking young man, the Lord managed to convince me quickly. "OK, James," I found myself saying, "I'll give you ten minutes."

The ten minutes turned out to be forty minutes as we sat alone in the television room composing a beautiful four-page letter to his mom. At first all he wanted to ask her was to send some soap and toothpaste, but through some gentle coaxing I helped him include a lot more information and detail that a mother needed to hear about her son.

In the following weeks I could never quite figure out why all the services I held were attended by almost every kid in camp, Catholics as well as Protestants. James, the constant pain in my side, was now a model participant at every activity I conducted. Before, he would stop kids from taking an active part; now I had the feeling he was in a quiet way forcing them to participate. Kids who would normally not share and read the Scriptures readily did so when asked by James. He kept any unruly kid from disrupting services and seemed to be mesmerized by every word that I spoke. This really puzzled me and I couldn't figure out why.

The answer came after prayer when I asked the Lord, "What is going on?"

"Don't just read and preach the Gospel. Live it!" came the reply.

When I realized that James had a need (he wanted to write a letter) and I met his need - that was the thing that made the difference in his life. It was as if a light had been turned on in my head and I all of a sudden saw things in a new way. Actions can speak a lot louder than words when it comes to the Gospel.

My ministry to the kids in detention quickly focused on their needs, physical as well as spiritual.

The principles I learned in detention ministry I try to apply in everything I now do. So thanks to James for helping me realize that an effective ministry has to identify and meet needs; and most importantly, not only do I have to preach the Gospel, I have to live it.

CHAPTER 4

CATHOLIC

OR

CHRISTIAN

Any Catholic who instructs other Catholics cannot separate the Lord from the Church or the Sacraments that He established.

Chapter 4

Catholic or Christian?

Once I sought help from my own parish for people to volunteer and teach religious instruction to the young inmates. One particular middle-aged lady, who had just completed her certification through the local

Archdiocese, enthusiastically responded. Innocently I turned over a weekly class that I had already formed, which was made up of 20 young men from 12 to 16 years old. The purpose of the class was to get the young men prepared so that they could make their first Holy Communion while still in camp.

A few weeks later, I happened to visit the camp during the time of her class. I thought I would look in on everyone to see how things were. To my surprise, there were less than half the original group of boys gathered in the room with the lady volunteer. When I asked about the others, she informed me that they had all dropped out and were no longer part of the group. This puzzled me, as I knew most of the boys pretty well, and they had all seemed anxious to complete their religious instruction. Leaving the room, I headed out onto the athletic field to see if I could find any familiar faces among the boys who were there playing.

"Hi, Mr. Scotty!" shouted one young Mexican boy from across the field. Looking over I motioned for him to come to me.

"Carlos, what's this I hear - you're no longer going to the instruction class; why not?"

The smile quickly vanished from Carlos's face as he nervously replied, "I don't want to be Catholic any more, Mr. Scotty! I want to be Christian!"

"What makes you think that there is any difference between being Catholic or Christian, Carlos?"

The young man cast his glance down towards the ground and shifted uncomfortably from one foot to another. "The lady - she says there is a difference, and I have decided now that I want to be a Christian," was his reply.

"What lady are you talking about, Carlos? And could you explain the whole situation to me very slowly?" I asked somewhat confused.

As Carlos began to relate to me his story, other young men who had previously attended the same class joined us. They all confirmed Carlos's account of what had happened, which basically was as follows: During an instruction class, one of the boys asked the lady volunteer if a Catholic was permitted to marry a Christian.

The lady's reply was, "No! Catholics are not allowed to marry Christians."

Another youth asked the lady, "What is the difference between Catholics and Christians?"

Her response was, "Catholics believe in Mary and the Rosary, and Christians believe in Jesus and the Bible."

After the class, Carlos and the other boys agonized over the dilemma of whether to be Catholic or Christian. Most of them were getting into the Bible seriously for the first time in their lives, and they really felt they were finding answers for themselves as they searched the Scriptures every day. All the boys said it was a difficult decision for them to come to but were all sure they had made the right choice. Before leaving, I asked them to promise me that they would come to our weekly Communion service the following day, as I had something very important to tell them. Next I went back to speak to the lady volunteer.

We talked privately in the parking lot outside the camp away from the main buildings. I explained to the lady my conversation with Carlos, and asked her if what he said was true. She confirmed everything just as Carlos had related it, so I asked her if she thought that it might be possible for a Catholic to be a practicing Christian. Her reply was, "Never!"

I then suggested to her that she enroll herself in the parish adult inquiry class and learn more about the Church and its teachings. Afterwards, she could see me and we could discuss the possibilities of her coming back to volunteer at camp. But until such times as she had learned more of her Catholic faith, I could not permit her to continue teaching the boys.

Angrily the lady reminded me that she had a teaching certificate issued by the Archdiocese, and I hadn't. She suggested that I should be the one to go back to school and threatened to go straight to our pastor and tell him of my insulting remarks.

I'm glad to say that I had a very understanding pastor who reminded her that I was the person in charge, and that my request of her was in order and should be taken seriously. She did not take my advice or the pastor's, and she never again came back to the camp.

My whole point in relating this story is - if we are not aware of the Church's teachings, how can we properly instruct others? On the other side of the spectrum, I recently read a book published by "A Catholic Evangelical Community," whose special calling is to bring the good news of Jesus Christ to Catholics. Their book, 120 pages in length, and I assume aimed at Catholics (although it didn't specifically mention it), encouraged the reader to a personal relationship with the Lord. But nowhere in the book did they mention or encourage the reader to practice their Catholic faith, be active in their parish community, or frequent the sacraments. All of which is very important for us in order to grow spiritually as Catholics. If any Catholic individual or group attempts to lead or instruct other fellow Catholics, surely they cannot separate the Lord from the Church or the sacraments that He established.

CHAPTER 5

MOUSE AND THE GOSPEL

"Make it your practice to store up for yourselves heavenly treasure where neither moths nor rust corrode nor thieves steal. Remember, where your treasure is, there your heart is also."
Matthew 6: 20 -21

Chapter 5

The Mouse and the Gospel

For the weekly Communion services at camp, I tried to take from the Sunday readings a passage that would seem applicable or easy for the boys to relate to. Rarely did I manage to put together a lesson plan without difficulty, but when I read the Scriptures for the coming week, a number of brilliant ideas and associations filled my mind. I got so excited that I could hardly wait to give my scriptural talk that weekend. I was thoroughly convinced that I would be able to make the Gospel point on "sharing God's gifts" crystal clear.

When I arrived at camp I felt a tinge of confidence, knowing that I was well-prepared to conduct a good service. The Duty Counselor made the remark that quite a large number of boys had requested to attend the Catholic service that week, and if I wanted all of them, he would open up the gymnasium for us. Well, this seemed like a confirmation from the Lord. I felt good; more kids wanted to come to the service, so I readily said, "OK, I'll take them all."

Fifty kids and I marched over to the gym. Once inside, we arranged our chairs in a huge circle in the middle of the floor. The boys were on their best behavior and I had little trouble getting them to genuinely participate. While saying the Creed together I noticed that a small "plump" field mouse was getting some attention from the boys as it scampered the length of the far wall of the gym. Then as we prayed the Confiteor, the same little mouse made another appearance; this time it scurried past quite close to our circle. This caused some muffled giggles, but when the mouse ran and disappeared through the doorway heading to the back store room, there were muffled cheers of encouragement and whispered cries of approval from the boys. I quickly reminded everyone that this was a prayer service and we should not let things distract us. Next we took turns reading the Scriptures - the Gospel passage relating "not to store up earthly treasures." One of the boys had just started reading when the little mouse came back again. This time the mouse ran right into the middle of our circle, sat down, and surveyed us for about thirty seconds. The boys obviously enjoyed the whole spectacle and for the first time I noticed that they noiselessly communicated some affection towards the little mouse as it sat within our circle. When the little guy decided to scurry back towards the store room, I quietly asked the Lord to keep His little creature away from the service.

After the Scriptures were read, and before giving my talk, I asked if everyone understood the passage. Everyone nodded as if to indicate "Yes."

Just as I was about to begin my talk, the field mouse reappeared and trotted boldly back into the middle of our circle. He again sat down and began to groom himself, unaware of my intense desire to have him leave quickly.

The boys on the other hand loved the whole incident. They all sat perfectly still and motioned each other not to make a sound lest the little guy be scared away. Frustrated, I sat there watching the overweight mouse go through his whole routine; grooming his face, legs, and tail. After what seemed like an eternity, the mouse decided to wander back towards the store room. He quietly vanished through the doorway leaving all of us sitting silently in our circle. There were no cheers for the mouse this time as he left, but I did notice the boys were all deep in thought. I figured I would give them a minute to collect themselves before I presented my talk. But before I could begin, one of the boys remarked, "It's true what the Bible says. We shouldn't store up anything here." The other boys all nodded in agreement and before I could say anything, they began an open discussion about not hoarding and sharing all of the things that God gives us. In their exchanges I heard the mouse being referred to several times, and this confused me. There was obviously an inside story that I wasn't getting, especially when one of the boys named Jimmy remarked that he felt God had sent the mouse to our service to remind them of the Scripture we had just read.

Just as I was about to ask for an explanation, out came the mouse again onto the floor of the gym. Again the little guy scampered into our circle, and just as before, he sat and began to groom himself, perfectly happy and quite unconcerned about the circle of humans that surrounded him.

Feeling somewhat frustrated, I asked Jimmy, "How could God send a mouse to convey a Gospel truth?" To my surprise he eagerly related the following story:

Six months ago, two hundred chocolate bars were donated to the prison authorities with instructions that they had to be freely distributed to the young inmates. The authorities decided instead to keep the candy locked up in the refrigerator in the gym store room until Christmas. Now that Christmas was drawing near, someone opened the refrigerator to check on the candy bars and found all of them gone. They had vanished into thin air. The only evidence left was some chewed wrappers, a small hole in the back of the refrigerator, and tell-tale signs that mice had invaded the padlocked refrigerator.

Our discussion was lively as we shared how God's Word applied to that situation. I marveled at the insights the boys had and the fantastic suggestions they came up with on how they could apply the same principles to their lives. Their openness and understanding as to what God was telling us through the Scriptures was fantastic.

As I drove home that day I thanked the Lord for sending His little mouse to the service. Although I didn't get a chance to share my "wonderful thoughts" with the boys, it was OK. I figured the mouse did a far better job of communicating the point God wanted to make.

CHAPTER 6

A ROSARY FOR ROBERT

"You are my rock and my fortress; for your name's sake you will lead and guide me. You will free me from the snare they set for me."

Psalm 31: 4

Chapter 6

A Rosary for Robert

Robert, an outgoing and constantly smiling fifteen year-old, looked very much out of place in the Juvenile Detention Camp. His white freckled face and rugged "Tom Sawyer" features contrasted with the sea of black and brown faces that shared the overcrowded detention facility. I first met him as he was serving his second term in juvenile detention. He always spoke politely to me when I visited the camp, but never once did he respond to my invitations to join the Bible study or attend Church services. His favorite reply was always, "I'm not a Catholic." Despite not coming to any service, Robert did keep pestering me for a Rosary. "Why do you want a Rosary? I asked.

"Because I want to get close to God," he replied.

When I asked, "Do you know how to pray the Rosary?"

He sheepishly shook his head saying, "I just know if I had a Rosary I would feel close to God."

It seemed "too good" a reason for wanting a Rosary, so when he refused to join in on any of the church-related activities, I decided not to give him one. Previously, Rosaries were misused by kids at camp as gang symbols and certain-colored Rosaries were worn in a particular fashion to indicate gang connections or affiliations. It was for this reason that I decided that Rosaries would go only to those kids I thought knew how to pray and use them properly.

Every week without fail, whenever Robert would spot me, he would call out to me from across the athletic field or wherever he was and ask, "Mr. Scotty, do you have my Rosary?"

Always I would reply, "No! '"

Later during my personal prayer time, I started to find Robert popping up in my meditations. Always he would be calling for his Rosary. At first I quickly dismissed these incidents, but as they progressively became more and more frequent, I began to wonder what this all meant. Then one night I dreamt the same incident; Robert calling out to me for a Rosary. The dream was so vivid that it woke me up at three o'clock in the morning. I remember sitting straight up in bed and saying out loud, "OK, ok, I'll bring you a Rosary."

It just so happened that the next evening was my night for one-to-one counseling with the boys. I was determined not to do anything before seeing Robert first so I could give him a Rosary, thinking this would end his constant intrusion into my prayer life and dreams. The Duty Officer did not know where Robert was but suggested I walk over to the gymnasium and see if he was there playing basketball. It was winter time and dark as I made my way across the deserted athletic field. The gym, a big building situated near the chain-link perimeter fence, stood shrouded in darkness except for a slash of faint light from a weak overhead electric light bulb that half-lit the front entrance. There was no sign of a soul as I made my way towards it, then as I drew near I noticed the figure of someone standing nervously in the shadow area of the recessed doorway. It was a boy with his jacket collar pulled up around his face and his black stocking cap pulled tightly down over his head leaving only the eyes barely visible.

"Robert!" I exclaimed in surprise, "What are you doing standing out here?"

An obviously nervous boy answered, "I came out for a drink." Then he proceeded to slowly and deliberately drink from the noisy water font that was next to the doorway.

As I looked past Robert, I noticed the faint outline of a boy's head spying on us from the far end of the building.

"Who is that?" I asked as the head quickly popped back behind the gym wall.

"I dunno," replied Robert not even bothering to look in that direction. "What do you want anyway?" continued Robert as he stood up and wiped his mouth with his coat sleeve.

"I've come to give you this," I said as I watched Robert's eyes grow as big as saucers as he observed me take out a lovely white Rosary from my jacket pocket.

The look on his face was genuine astonishment. "Why did you bring this tonight?" he stammered.

"Because I believe God wanted you to have it," I answered.

"But why did you bring it tonight?" repeated Robert.

I looked at him a bit surprised and answered, "You have been asking me for months for a Rosary and when I finally do bring it to you, and you ask me why?" I placed the Rosary into Robert's cupped hands and watched as he gently caressed the Crucifix.

How long we stood there in the dark I don't know. Suddenly, the quiet was shattered by the yelling and screaming of Duty Personnel to the effect that some kids had just scaled the outer fence. Within minutes all the boys in the camp were frantically lined up and counted. The three boys that were found to be missing were apprehended half an hour later, not far from camp.

Looking back over the situation, I believe that Robert was planning to scale the fence that night, but my bringing him the Rosary stopped that from happening.

Robert became a model inmate at camp and went home early because of good behavior. In camp, he constantly wore the white Rosary around his neck. Every now and then he would remark, "God is still looking after me," and gratefully pat the Crucifix attached to his Rosary.

For me, the incident with Robert is a constant reminder that God does speak in many ways and that I should be open always to hearing Him.

CHAPTER 7

PABLO'S LUCKY MEDAL

*"Be my rock of refuge, a stronghold to give me safety.
You are my rock and my fortress; for your
name's sake you will lead and guide me."*
Psalm 31: 3-4

Chapter 7

Pablo's Lucky Medal

Pablo, a portly, lovable, street-smart Hispanic youngster, had somehow managed to secure the self-appointed position of "Camp Altar Boy." He was a cheerful and talkative youth who turned out to be a great help and performed an invaluable service for me in my duties at the detention camp. Meeting him for the first time, his warm, friendly personality gave the impression that he was totally reformed – a model inmate, but I quickly learned that behind the big disarming smile, he was not the perfect angel. He wasn't a bad boy either; it's just that you had to make sure you got "all" the matches back from him after he lit the candles and always recounted any items you brought with you before leaving. He had served and assisted me for eight months and was now getting ready to go home in a couple of weeks.

Late one evening as I made an unscheduled stop at camp to pick up my mail, I was shocked to find Pablo sitting in a chair in the main office with his hands behind him, shackled in handcuffs. He looked totally dejected and for the first time since I had known him, he didn't greet me with a smile.

"What's up, Pablo?" I asked as I noticed a small bruise near his right eye.

Before Pablo could say anything, the Senior Duty Officer Mr. Green (or "Mean Joe" as the kids referred to him) spoke rather sharply to me. "He's off-limits to you. Pablo's in big trouble this time... he's been fighting."

"Can I speak with him?" I asked.

"Mean Joe," who was never in a good mood, just shook his head indicating "no way;" then barked, "He'll be out of here in five minutes and on his way to solitary. I've already called for the wagon and it's on its way."

My head went spinning when I heard the Duty Officer mention solitary. That means that Pablo would be transferred immediately to another facility, usually a stricter detention camp, and confined in a solitary cell. When that happens, the inmate usually receives an added "stiff" sentence. A thousand thoughts whirled through my mind as I realized that I would never see Pablo again after this evening, and that his plans to go home in a couple of weeks were now completely shattered.

"Can I at least pray with him?" I sort of pleaded with Mr. Green.

"It will do you no good," he responded, "but go ahead and make it quick."

Turning to Pablo, who never raised his eyes from the floor, I pulled up a chair next to him and sat down. I reached behind and took hold of his hands. I remember thinking, as I felt the cold steel handcuffs, "I've never before prayed with someone who had handcuffs on." But the firm grip of Pablo's cold and nervous hands, as they desperately grabbed for mine, quickly brought my mind back into focus.

"Help me. I'm scared Mr. Scotty. I didn't start no fight. I don't want to go to Solitary," pleaded Pablo.

Although I sympathized and believed every word he uttered, I also found it extremely difficult to pray with Pablo. My mind was filled with all the things I so desperately wanted to say to him. I wanted to say thanks and also let him know he was such a great help to me and how much I appreciated his friendship. My prayer was fragmented as I desperately searched for the right words to say, knowing that he needed to hear words of comfort and encouragement now more than ever. Adding to my slightly confused state, Pablo kept a vice-like grip on my hands as he desperately clung to me; this caused me to interrupt my prayer and ask him to ease up a little with his grip. Reluctantly, he did so.

"Time's up," exclaimed Green.

"Can I have a Bible?" asked Pablo in a hushed voice.

I looked at the Officer and relayed the question. "Can he have a Bible?"

"Nope! He goes exactly as is. No Bible; all his gear stays here and will be forwarded later." replied Green.

Observing the pitiful look on Pablo's face I tried to bargain with Mr. Green. "How about if I give him MY Bible?"

Again the response was, "Nope!"

As I looked into Pablo's eyes I could see his pain and desperation.

"I need something, Mr. Scotty," pleaded Pablo.

Putting my hand in my pocket I pulled out a small religious Medal. Holding it up for the Duty Officer to see I asked, "Can I give him this?"

Mr. Green, who was getting a little irritated with my bargaining, looked at the Medal and then at me. "He goes as is. Anything you give him will be taken from him the minute they arrive to pick him up."

Not quite sure what he really meant, I inquired, "You mean it's OK for me to give Pablo this Medal?

"If the Medal is in his pocket when the wagon arrives, it will be taken from him," replied Green as he slowly turned his back on us and began fumbling through a file cabinet drawer.

Taking the response to mean that it was OK, I slipped the Medal into Pablo's trouser pocket. The look on Pablo's face conveyed a silent message of gratitude.

My heart was heavy during the drive home that night as I thought of my little friend. He wasn't a fighter or a bully and for him to be involved in an altercation with another kid was almost impossible for me to believe.

Fighting is not tolerated at camp and the guilty party or parties are swiftly and severely dealt with and removed – never to return. So with bitter reluctance I resigned myself to the fact that I would not be seeing Pablo's smiling face anymore.

The next morning when I arrived at camp I almost died of shock. There was Pablo, with the biggest smile on his face I've ever seen, going about his normal duties – setting up the altar for our morning service.

"Pablo!" I exclaimed, "What happened?"

Pablo, obviously very happy, just couldn't wait to answer me. "Mr. Scotty," he blurted, "I didn't go to Solitary."

"I can see that, Pablo, but why not?" I asked.

"The wagon that was on its way to pick me up broke down, so it never came," said Pablo as he seemingly bounced with joy. "They couldn't get it fixed and they didn't have another wagon to send in its place."

"What did Mr. Green say?" I asked.

"Mean Joe was very, very mad," said Pablo as he continued his story. "Instead of going home at midnight, he had to stay until three o'clock in the morning. He waited for the wagon, but it didn't come. They told Mean Joe that if he still wanted to send me to Solitary, he would have to stay over until at least eight o'clock. He didn't want to stay so he turned me over to his relief, Mr. Wilson. Mr. Wilson is a good guy. He believed I didn't start the fight and let me off with a warning. Aren't I lucky, Mr. Scotty?"

"You sure are, Pablo, and I'm glad things worked out OK for you," I said as I gave him a big hug.

"Everybody says I'm lucky. It's like a miracle because nobody ever got out of going to Solitary… I'm the only one!" said Pablo all puffed up with pride." I bet it was that lucky Medal you gave me that brought me the luck."

Fishing the Medal from his pocket, he held it out for me to see. "Does this Medal have a name?" he asked.

"Yes, Pablo," I smiled, "it's called a Miraculous Medal."

CHAPTER 8

The
BANDIT STORY

"I ask that your minds may be opened to see His light, so that you will know what is the hope to which He has called you, how rich are the wonderful blessings He promises His people."
Ephesians 1: 18

Chapter 8

The Bandit Story

There is a constant flow of hopeless and dejected youth that go through the ever-revolving doors of the juvenile detention system. Seeing their young faces week after week would prompt me to ask myself, "How can I reach as many of them as possible and how can I communicate to them some hope?"

Wednesday nights were usually field game nights and that's when I would endeavor to spend an hour or so trying to meet the new kids in this unorganized and informal setting. But meeting new kids while out on the athletic field wasn't always easy; as most seemed more interested in playing than taking time out to talk to some unfamiliar guy that just happened to be wandering around. What I needed was an attraction that would divert their attention from the games to me. But what? After talking over a few ideas with one of the Camp Counselors we came up with a thought. What if I were to bring my dog with me one night?

Taking my large, slightly overweight German Shepherd dog named Bandit into the camp was sort of a calculated gamble, as there was no way we could figure out beforehand how the kids would react. Bandit I knew was no problem as he loved kids and liked being the center of attention, but his size and looks did cause some people to cautiously stop or nervously step aside whenever he approached.

Bandit's first visit, to put it mildly, was a wild success. Every kid stopped playing their particular game to come and check the big dog out. Some approached him very cautiously while others just came up and threw their arms around him and lovingly hugged him. I figured Bandit must have thought he had died and gone to heaven, as a hundred or so youth fussed over and petted him for more than an hour. He relished every minute of it. He patiently sat and shook hands with almost every kid, then wandered aimlessly among them and leaned lazily and happily against anyone who just happened to volunteer to scratch or rub his back or ears.

Every kid wanted to know the dog's name, where he came from, and what tricks he could he do. They were quite surprised when I told them that Bandit was a retired movie star. He had done three television pictures for Walt Disney Productions when he was younger. I also explained that I used to be an animal trainer and had found Bandit, then an unwanted bag of skin and bones, abandoned in an animal shelter where he had been discarded by his previous owner with the implicit instructions that he had to be "put to sleep."

Of course they wanted Bandit to do some tricks, which he did, and this thoroughly delighted them. So by an overwhelming vote of approval, a new companion joined me each week for my regular Wednesday night field visits.

Bandit would casually wander around the athletic field and nuzzle up to kids as if they were old friends. The kids for their part took delight in acknowledging him and introducing him to other kids by having him go through his now regular routine of "shake" and "speak." The dog seemed to have a sixth sense at locating the ones who were despondent or loners. He would instinctively seek them out, nuzzle up to them, and in no time have them happily rubbing his big fur frame.

Every week, at least twice, I would be approached by a young, thinly-built black youth named Anthony and some other boys and asked to tell the story of how I found Bandit abandoned in the animal shelter, how he was just one day away from being put to sleep, and how he was rescued and given another chance at life. This storytelling would go on every week without fail.

After awhile, I was beginning to believe that taking Bandit into the camp wasn't such a great idea after all. The dog's life story was getting too much attention and no matter how much I tried to change the subject, the boys kept coming back to it. It seemed as if that's all they wanted to talk about. What should I do? Already I was tired of repeating the story and would try and skip some of the features, but the boys, especially Anthony, would instantly correct me and remind me of them. At times, Anthony or one of the other boys would take it upon themselves to take over my storytelling and complete it, being very careful to leave out none of the details.

One night after reluctantly telling the "Bandit Story" to Anthony and a group of kids, I called Anthony aside and impatiently asked him, "Why do you keep asking me to tell you the story of how I found Bandit?"

With eyes as big as saucers, Anthony looked at me with a surprised innocence before answering, "Mr. Scotty, we need to hear it all the time."

"Why, Anthony? You've heard it a dozen times; that should be enough," I responded dryly.

"Well Bandit was in the dog pound, right?" he asked as he looked at me questioningly.

"That's right!" I muttered reluctantly.

If Anthony sensed my slight impatience he never showed it; he just continued talking to me as if I were being told the story of Bandit for the first time. "The dog pound is a prison for dogs and Bandit was in there. He also was all skin and bones. That means nobody cared for him or what happened to him or nothing. The person that owned him didn't even want him around. Bandit's only crime was that nobody loved or truly cared for him and for that he was put on death row. He only had one day left when you gave him a second chance, right?"

"That's right, Anthony!" I quietly responded.

Anthony looked at me a bit puzzled, as if he were surprised that I didn't know the real reason behind the Bandit story. "That's why we need to hear the story over and over again. If a dog that nobody wanted or loved could be given a second chance and make it, then maybe we can too."

When it finally dawned on me the real reason for them to hear the story, I swallowed hard, put my arm around Anthony and gave him a thankful hug. "You're right, Anthony! You do need to hear the Bandit story again and again and I'll be glad to tell you or any of the other boys anytime you wish."

Anthony scrutinized me a bit warily. "You won't leave any parts out, will you?"

I gave him a reassuring smile. "I promise from now on I won't."

Looking really serious, Anthony commented, "You know Mr. Scotty, all us kids are just like Bandit, and seeing him here every week and hearing his story over and over again gives us hope."

"I know Anthony," I replied as he ran off and joined his friends on the field. I don't think he heard my final comment which was a little muffled and apologetic. "Thanks for reminding me."

CHAPTER 9

A

DECISION FOR CARLOS

"May He grant what is in your heart

and fulfill your every plan.

May we shout for joy at your victory

And raise the standards in the name

Of our God:"

Psalm 20:5-6

Chapter 9

A Decision for Carlos

Carlos, a tall, muscular sixteen year-old, had already spent over half of his young life in and out of various detention facilities. He had a violent temper that took very little to trigger and was probably the main cause of most of his incarcerations. Often I heard probation staff members refer to him as a "career criminal" and in their opinion, someone who would someday probably end up on death row. My brief encounters with Carlos always left me with the impression that he was an angry young man and that violence was the only way he knew how to resolve any conflict. He never seemed interested in talking with me and once remarked that he and I had nothing in common, so I pretty much left him alone.

One day after a Communion service at camp I was asked by the Duty Counselor to speak privately with Carlos.

The Counselor told me that Carlos's father had died the day before, the innocent victim of a drive-by shooting in East Los Angeles. Carlos had taken the news of his father's death quietly and this caused concern among staff members. Withdrawing from everyone, the boy didn't express any normal emotional reactions and refused to talk with anyone about his father's death. Carlos did ask to be furloughed so that he could attend his father's funeral, but his relatives made it clear that they did not want him there, so the request was denied.

Later I met Carlos on the only private spot available to us, the empty baseball field. He and I sat down on an old wooden bench behind the baseline.

"Why did my dad have to die?" he asked.

I really struggled for the answer. "I honestly don't know," I haltingly responded.

"Why did God have my dad killed?"

Again I felt unable to give a proper answer and mumbled something like, "Well, I don't think God wanted your dad shot or purposely planned to have him…"

Carlos angrily interrupted. "Then why did God permit it to happen?" he demanded as he looked directly into my eyes for the first time.

"God didn't plan your dad's death," I responded as I looked into his piercing brown eyes that revealed anger and pain. "Maybe I don't have the answers you're looking for, Carlos, but I'd like to pray with you to God for them."

He shook his head, declining the invitation to pray, stood up and looked off aimlessly into the distance. "Right now," he said coldly just loud enough for me to hear, "I don't feel like praying." He then turned and walked away, leaving me with a feeling of being totally useless and alone.

In the days and weeks that followed, the brooding Carlos was watched closely for any signs that would communicate his intentions. Most everyone I talked with at the detention camp figured it was only a matter of time before he tried to break out and take some sort of revenge. He was likened to a time bomb and everyone was openly guessing when it would go off.

Almost a month later the startling news came through that Carlos's mother had just died in a hospital. It seems that she had been a sickly young woman in her thirties who had battled cancer for quite some time. Despite requests from aunts and uncles that Carlos not be allowed out for the funeral, the authorities this time decided to grant Carlos's request.

Shackled and cuffed, he was permitted to witness his mother's funeral a little ways apart from the other mourners. The only other surviving family member, a 12-year-old sister named Teresa, was forbidden by other relatives to speak with Carlos. Their only communication that day in the cemetery was a few stolen glances.

Later I was asked to speak with Carlos, and again we met out in the deserted baseball field. "Why did my mom have to die?" he asked in a soft, deliberate voice.

"I don't know why she had to die, Carlos. The only thing I do know is that some people twice your age could not go through what you are going through right now."

Carlos looked at me a little puzzled.

"I understand your mom was in great pain for a long time with the cancer."

He nodded his head and looked away, not wanting me to see the tears that welled up in his eyes when I mentioned his mother.

Why I spoke so firmly I don't know, but I found myself emphatically saying, "All I can tell you now is that she is not in any more pain and is now reunited with your dad. Your mom, if you believe in heaven, is extremely happier now than she has ever been in her life on earth. God would not allow both your parents to die without giving you the grace to go through this very painful ordeal. They say a crisis is always a turning point in people's lives. Good or bad, people make decisions at crucial times that ultimately will affect their whole lives. How you decide to react to this crisis will shape your future. Right now Jesus lovingly extends a special grace to you, and it's up to you to either accept it or reject it. I'm told your relatives had all given up on you years ago and everyone here is taking bets as to when you will crack up and go over the wall. The decision is yours, Carlos. Although you may now be a rejected orphan, there's a God who loves you and will never reject you. He wants to be a father to you. So there's no need to go through life alone.

He has the answers you're seeking." I looked at Carlos to see if anything I said got through to him, but he just stared at the ground.

"I have to go," he said as he quietly stood up.

"Would you like to pray?" I inquired.

"No," replied Carlos as he slowly wandered off, leaving me in the middle of the deserted field.

Later that evening my mind was filled with thoughts of quitting the juvenile detention ministry. I figured I was doing more damage than good to the kids I was trying to help - Carlos being the case in point. So it was with a reluctant spirit that I returned to camp the following day.

"Carlos wants to see you," yelled the Duty Counselor as I came through the main security gate.

"What for?" I asked.

The Counselor just shook his head, indicating he didn't know.

Out on the field I nervously sat on the bench watching Carlos walk out to meet me. I had mixed feelings. Already I had decided, this time I'll just keep quiet and let him do the talking. Silently I prayed that God would help me keep my big mouth shut.

Carlos sat down beside me and nervously cleared his throat before speaking. "I have already made my decision," he began, "but I want to ask you to help me make sure I do it right."

His opening remark made my heart jump and lodge in my throat. Before I could get any words out, Carlos continued, "Would you help me pray to God?"

"Sure," I blurted as I reached out and took his hands and cradled them in mine.

"How do I do it?" he asked in an innocent boyish manner.

"Just talk to God the same way you're talking to me, Carlos."

He shifted nervously, bowed his head slightly, and began to speak slowly and deliberately as we continued to hold hands. "Dear Jesus, I know I've done a lot of bad things in my life and I'm sorry. Last night I made a decision to change, and as Mr. Scotty is my witness, I'm asking You to help me. I know a lot of people won't believe I want to change and it will even take years for some of them to believe me, but that's OK. Help me with that grace Mr. Scotty said You give people. And could you help my little sister too, because she must be feeling the same kind of hurts and things inside that I've been feeling. There's a lot of tough business I have to take care of, but if You help me, I know I can take care of it. Look after my mom and dad and tell them not to worry about Teresa, my little sister. I promise I'll take care of her, just wait and see."

I was still in a state of shock when Carlos looked at me and asked, "Is it OK now to ask God to be my Father?"

I nodded and tried to say yes, but the word stuck in my throat.

Carlos again bowed his head and squeezed my hands tightly as he prayed, "Dear God, could You be my Father… I think I would like that… do You need another son?"

By this time tears had welled up in my eyes, trickled down my cheeks, and were now dropping freely on our clasped hands.

Carlos, once he realized what was happening, looked at me a bit surprised.

"It's OK, Carlos," I assured him, "they are tears of joy."

I then encouraged him to continue his prayer, a prayer that not only asked God to be his Father but also a lovely prayer requesting that Mary be his Mother.

Carlos finished out his time at camp with no blemish to his record. When it was time for him to go home, no relatives could be found that was willing to take him into their home, so he was transferred to a Youth Authority Camp where he would work and fight forest fires until he reached eighteen.

I talked with Carlos before he left camp and expressed my sadness at him not finding a home among his relatives. He just smiled and reminded me that it will take years to convince people that he has had a true change of heart. He hugged me as he left camp that day, happy with the knowledge and thoroughly convinced that God would eventually get him to the goal that he had set his heart on being reunited with his little sister.

CHAPTER 10

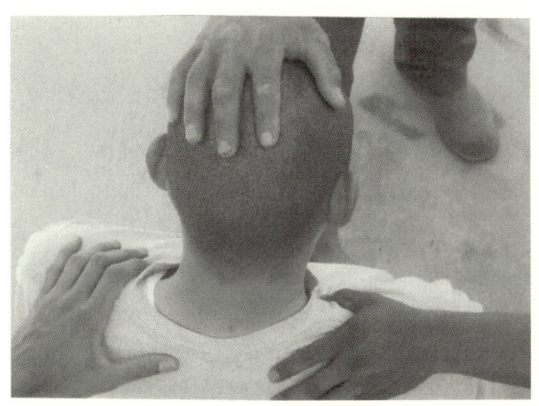

A
PRAYER
FOR CRAZY

*"If two of you join your voices on earth
to pray for anything whatever,
it shall be granted you by my Father in heaven.
Where two or three are gathered in my name,
there am I in their midst."*
　　　　　　　　　　Matthew 18:19

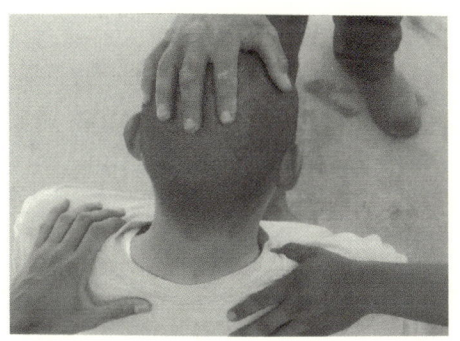

Chapter 10

A Prayer for Crazy

About two dozen spirited juvenile inmates noisily scrambled into the detention camp's TV room and began rearranging the wooden chairs that were scattered aimlessly around the small drab room. I scanned the group to see if there were any new boys and spotted a couple of new faces. Old or new faces, it made no difference; they all religiously had to make minor, noisy adjustments in the placement and position of their chairs before they sat down. I watched and waited patiently for them to settle down before beginning our weekly Bible study, and as usual, the last to settle himself was "Crazy," a slim-built fourteen year-old Hispanic boy. I don't recall his real name, but everyone including myself and the staff, addressed him as "Crazy," which he seemingly liked and readily answered to. He was a likable young man who had obvious mental problems. Crazy's erratic actions, I was told, and his inability to hold lengthy conversations were results of years of an addiction to paint sniffing. This had damaged and gravely affected his mental functions. Normal conversations with him were almost impossible as he had difficulty remembering or following a train of thought for more than sixty seconds.

The main point I was trying to press home to the boys during our Bible study that evening was the power of prayer. Especially the power of united prayer. We read and discussed Matthew 18: 19-20, Matthew 21:22 and other Scriptures relating to prayer.

While I was emphasizing that there was nothing impossible for God, one of the fresh-faced young boys mockingly interrupted. "If you really believe all that stuff you're telling us," he challenged me, "then why don't you pray for Crazy?"

Feeling somewhat put on the spot, I glanced over at Crazy and asked if he wanted us to pray for him. "I'd like that," he happily stated.

Motioning the boys to gather around Crazy so that we could lay hands on him, I then asked, "What you want us to pray for?"

"I want God to heal my brain and help me kick the habit of sniffing paint," requested Crazy in a childlike manner.

There was immediate snickering among the boys.

One of the boys, his face taut with anger, verbally lashed out at me. "You have no right to do this! We all know there is no hope for Crazy, and what you're doing here is wrong."

"What am I doing?" I asked him.

"You're giving Crazy false hope. All of us know there's no cure for him. You should be reported to the authorities!" Kneeling in front of Crazy, I looked up at all the kids standing around him. "Who believes that God can help Crazy?" I questioned.

There was an uneasy silence with some more muffled jeering laughter.

"OK," I replied, "Who believes that Crazy is too far gone and is beyond God's help?"

Most of the kids responded that they felt Crazy was a hopeless case.

After a brief survey, there were only five of us in the room who believed God could help Crazy. The five of us gathered around Crazy while the others observed. We prayed a simple prayer asking God to heal Crazy's mind and cure him of his addiction. It was a short prayer that took about two minutes.

Afterwards, everyone watched Crazy closely for any miraculous sign of healing. There was none! He left the TV room that evening showing no evidence of being cured; in fact he appeared to be functioning crazier than before.

As I drove home that night I was deeply troubled about how the evening Bible study concluded. Did I let things get out of hand? Did I push the power of prayer too much on the boys? Was I stretching their faith too far? Although I believed God could do all those things Crazy requested, the piercing words of the young, angry inmate kept haunting me all the way home. Was I giving the boys false hope? The more I reflected back over the "Crazy" incident, the more I began to wonder if maybe the young man was right.

A few days later on a Saturday morning, I was back at the camp for a Communion service. Again I stood and watched the young men scramble into the room and rearrange their chairs before being seated.

Crazy was acting very animated and got my attention real fast as he jumped up and down excitedly in his seat. "Mr. Scotty, Mr. Scotty, can I say something?"

Thinking it best to get him calmed down as quickly as possible, I agreed and called him over to stand next to me. Addressing the boys in the room, Crazy began to relate the following: "A few days ago, behind the gymnasium, I found a big paint can in the trash. The can still had some paint in it. When I looked around and found no one was watching, I tried to sniff the paint but I couldn't; I didn't want to. I thought maybe I was nervous because of being in detention camp, so I hid the can in the bushes. Later I went back and sat in the bushes with the can between my knees and I tried once more. Again I felt like I didn't want to sniff the paint, so I put it back in the bushes. All that night I began to worry because I love to sniff paint and this never happened to me before."

The atmosphere in the small room was electric. Everyone knew Crazy really well and this was the first time we had heard him intelligently relate any detailed sentences for more than a minute. The boys and I could only listen in sheer amazement as Crazy continued his story.

"The next day I went back to the paint and again I put the can between my knees and tried to force myself to sniff the fumes." Crazy shook his head in disbelief. "Same thing happened again – I didn't want to sniff." His eyes grew big and a smile flashed across his young face. "Then I remembered," he excitedly continued, "I remembered we all prayed and asked Jesus to help me kick the habit." With full animation and lots of energy, Crazy went through the motions of what he did next. "So I picked up that can of paint and threw it right over the fence as far as I could." Standing straight and looking at everyone in the eye, he quietly and clearly announced, "I know that I'm healed of sniffing paint and I know that Jesus will also heal my mind. So I just want to thank the Lord and all the guys that prayed for me." With that, he calmly sat down. You could have blown all of us over with a feather as we sat in total silence; not quite comprehending all that was said. It took a few minutes before I could gather myself together and begin the service.

That morning we discussed how Crazy was a person that some presumed had no chance of being healed, yet his story definitely confirmed the fact that THROUGH PRAYER ALL THINGS ARE POSSIBLE. Isn't it ironic that we all refer to him as "crazy," when he was the only one smart enough to ask God to do what some believe was impossible? Should not the "crazy ones" be those who mock or underestimate the power of prayer? Scripture reminds us "that with prayer all things are possible," and if we ever doubt that, we have a living example among us, a boy "crazy" enough to believe.

It was no surprise to me that our Communion service ran over that morning. Every one of the boys, even the fresh-faced kid and the one who challenged me at the Bible study, asked for and received individual prayer.

CHAPTER 11

A BENEDICTINE
BEHIND BARS

If anyone considers himself religious and yet does not keep a tight rein on his tongue, he deceives himself and his religion is worthless.

James 1:26

Chapter 11

A Benedictine Behind Bars

Kyle, a young man who had numerous brushes with the authorities for firearms violations and disturbing the peace, struggled to try and take care of business as he served a third term inside the juvenile facility. He anxiously shared with me after a Communion service that his uncontrollable problem was his nasty attitude - always quick to give a rapid-fire cutting reply to anyone who needled him.

"My biggest fault is my foul mouth. I just can't stop getting into trouble. People know how to get at me and no matter how hard I try, I keep on messing up."

As we talked a little more I discovered that there was something else that added to Kyle's frustration: his girl friend was pregnant and he didn't think he would be out in time for the baby's birth. This added disappointment did not help his attitude one bit.

Young inmates in the facility all wore blue shirts except for the trustees, who wore khaki shirts. Trustees were given special privileges, one of which would be a furlough to attend a child's birth if you were the father. Kyle tried desperately for the khaki shirt but somehow it always managed to elude him because of his undisciplined mouth.

"What can I do?" he asked as he grabbed my arm and held it tight. With a voice that whispered almost desperately resigned to hopelessness, he sighed, "I'll never get out of here if I keep on like this." (It's times like this I inwardly cry out to the Holy Spirit for help.)

I had no immediate response for Kyle except that I offered to pray with him. After a short prayer I continued our conversation by asking him when did he find it the most difficult to control his tongue. "The mornings are hell!! Always the mornings during movement or chow - that's when the guy's all get to me and that's when I mess up the most."

So the thought came to me, "Why not become a Benedictine!"

Kyle looked at me, bewildered, "A what?" he asked with an open mouth.

"A Benedictine," I replied, and began to explain that Benedictines are monks who live in a monastery that follow a strict rule of silence. In other words they don't speak until noon. I suggested to Kyle that he could turn the detention facility into a monastery and follow the Benedictine Rule. That way when some of the other kids needled him for a response, he would not react as before. Silence was going to be his new response.

Kyle thought for a moment and nodded his head in affirmation, "I like that!! Tell me more about this Benedictine stuff."

Well, I explained as best I could about the Benedictine Rule and impressed on Kyle that his mornings of silence could be a time of listening to God. I reminded him that prayer is a two way thing, us talking to God and God talking to us.

"If I don't say anything and everything is silence, how will I know what God is saying to me?" Kyle asked.

I suggested that he just be open to God speaking to him and not try to limit God in any way.

"OK, I'll try it!" said Kyle as he was motioned by the counselor to leave and get back to his dorm.

"I'll pray for you," was my final parting words as he exited the room.

A month later I visited the camp and spent some time alone with Kyle. "How is it going?" was my first question to him.

"Deacon Scotty, you're not going to believe all the stuff I have to tell you. It was the hardest thing for me not to say anything. I almost burst holding my tongue and not responding as normal." Then he proceeded to open the small Bible he carried in his back pocket and read to me the Scripture references he had earmarked. One by one he read from his little book verses:

Psalm 39:1, *"I will watch my ways and keep my tongue from sin; I will put a muzzle on my mouth as long as the wicked are in my presence."*

Psalm 15:3 *(he) who has no slander on his tongue, who does his neighbor no wrong and casts no slur on his fellowman,*

Psalm 71:24 *My tongue will tell of your righteous acts all day long.*

Proverbs 17:28 *Even a fool is thought wise if he keeps silent, and discerning if he holds his tongue.*

Kyle excitedly continued, "Every time I felt hopeless and near giving up I'd turn to God and He would always speak to me through the Bible. Listen to this one." Kyle quickly found the earmarked page and read the following passage:

Isaiah 50:4 *The Sovereign LORD has given me an instructed tongue, to know the word that sustains the weary. He wakens me morning by morning, wakens my ear to listen like one being taught.*

James 1:26 *If anyone considers himself religious and yet does not keep a tight rein on his tongue, he deceives himself and his religion is worthless.*

"God spoke to me through every Scripture that I found. Every time I felt angry and like bursting inside and wanting to make some nasty reply to someone, I'd find a quiet place and open up my Bible. I really feel that God is teaching me a new way of living and helping me to try and live like a Benedictine."

Kyle stopped as if in quiet thought, then asked, "Can a person really become a Benedictine if they're behind bars and in prison?"

I assured Kyle with a nod and a smile, "Of course! It doesn't matter where you are; if you follow and live the Benedictine Rule, I'm sure you would be considered a Benedictine."

"Cool!" was his reply. "I'm going to be the first Benedictine with a Khaki shirt."

In the following months, Kyle took on a whole new maturity and eventually graduated to his khaki shirt, which earned him a furlough to attend his son's birth. Our last conversation took place just before he left camp.

"Pray for me," he asked. "Pray that I make it!"

"You'll make it, Kyle!" I assured him. "Just keep doing what you've been doing and daily ask God for the graces you need to always follow the Benedictine Rule."

He looked at me with a serious eye-piercing glance. "That's the secret, eh?"

As I gave him an affirming, nod Kyle shook his head and laughed, "Cool...that's really cool!"

CHAPTER 12

EDWARD AND THE BROTHERS

Nervously Edward told me he had to "stick with the brothers," a term that I had never heard him use before.

Chapter 12

Edward and the Brothers

Edward, a thirteen year old black boy, was the nicest, well-mannered, and gentlest young man you'd ever care to meet. When I first met him in the juvenile detention facility I wanted to adopt him in the sense that I wanted to protect him from the negative influence of prison life. Whenever I commented to the authorities that I didn't think he belonged in a detention facility, no one believed me.

All of the camp counselors agreed that Edward, a rare exception to the rule, was certainly out of place among the criminal elements that served their time in juvenile detention. The records showed that he was arrested during a gang sweep by the police in East Los Angeles. Edward just happened to be in the wrong place at the wrong time, and for that he got six months as a first offender.

Edward, articulate and always polite, was born and raised Catholic. He knew all of his prayers and never missed a service. He was certainly a light in the dark world of detention. I looked forward to checking with Edward every time I visited the camp and in some cases made extra trips during the week to bring him a book or Rosary. Young men like Edward made going into the camp worthwhile. It gave you a sense of being needed and feeling useful. So any extra visits over and above the normal schedule were OK as they really appreciated it.

Then one Saturday morning I was surprised when Edward didn't turn up for religious services. When I inquired about him, I was told he was OK and will be attending the Baptist services from now on. Later I spoke with a nervous Edward privately and discovered the source of his change of heart and attitude. It seems the other black inmates decided that all the black brothers should band together and do things together as an outward show of their unity. And that meant going to the same religious services.

Nervously Edward told me he had to "stick with the brothers," a term that I had never heard him use before. Obviously he was under pressure from the other black inmates, and for him to not go along would be unwise.

For a whole week I agonized about his situation. The counselors tried talking to the young men about peer pressure and intimidation, but that never changed the situation. The brothers continued to stick together in sports, religion, and their free time. My prayers were constantly asking the Lord, "Why?" and what could I do to turn the situation around.

Two more weeks went by and still no change. My heart was breaking to see Edward, now timidly and fearfully subdued. He shouldn't have been in prison in the first place, and now he was caught up in a stupid "racial wagon-circling" episode.

Help finally came from the Lord in an unusual way. One morning at weekday Mass in my parish, while spending time before the Tabernacle, my prayers were interrupted by a young man who tapped my shoulder.

"Hi!" he began. "My name is Pete Wilson and the pastor said I should talk to you. Right now I'm beginning the Diaconate program in the Los Angeles Archdiocese and they recommend that I get involved in some outreach outside my parish. I was thinking detention ministry." I could have kissed him right there. Pete was African American, and after the shock wore off, I found out that he and his wife were also converts to the Catholic faith.

Next Saturday morning, I had Pete walk ahead of me into the detention facility as they announced "Religious Services" over the camp loudspeaker. Just as I thought – when they saw Pete, all the blacks automatically lined up to attend his service. There was quite a dilemma among the young black men after they found out that Pete was now going to conduct "Catholic" services. Edward was happy about the change and I quietly assured the other black young men that it was OK to attend the service with Pete. After all he was a brother, and brothers should stick together and support each other.

I'm happy to say that Edward never missed a Catholic service in camp before going home. That incident happened over twenty years ago and Deacon Pete and his wife are still ministering in that same detention facility to this very day.

CHAPTER 13

CHRISTMAS BANDIT

"Lord, I know he was just an old dog, but he meant the world to me and I loved him. Could you please let me know if he is with You?"

Chapter 13

Christmas Bandit

Each year, my wife Joi and I have been placing a little plastic statue of a dog next to the Infant Jesus in our Nativity Set at Christmas. Some people don't even notice; others politely remarked that a dog doesn't belong there.

Well, our little statue represents my dog Bandit; whether or not he belongs there, you can judge for yourself.

As you know, I found Bandit in an animal shelter where his owner had placed him to be disposed of. He looked like an undernourished Mexican street dog. That was the only thing he had going for him; he was exactly what I was searching for. At that time I was working for Walt Disney Productions on a film, and he fitted the description of the dog needed in the script. So the day before he was to be put to sleep, Bandit was rescued and began a new life and a career as a movie star. He was a "natural" and took directions very well. We were filming on the California and Mexican beaches. Bandit came alive as he romped and played, on and off camera, with the cast and crew. He won the hearts of everyone.

A special intimacy grew between Bandit and me; our relationship deepened more after several tragic accidents which almost took his life. The last mishap happened during another film. We were in Arizona. Bandit was badly bitten by a little animal called a coatimundi. The animal's razor-sharp teeth severed an artery inside Bandit's leg. From our remote location, two crew members and I made a mad dash across the Arizona desert, sixty miles to Tucson to a veterinarian. Holding

Bandit in my arms, I tried to suppress the steady flow of blood as he became limp. It was then that I began to realize that he had become a very important part of my life, and the thought of losing him almost broke my heart. I made the decision that if he pulled through this ordeal, I would retire him from the movies. Well he made it OK, thanks to a terrific Tucson veterinarian. After finishing that movie, I gave him to my sister and her family in Simi Valley, California. Bandit and I had to part company for awhile but at least I knew he'd be safe.

Domestic life agreed with him and he took his new "role" very seriously. The neighborhood kids all considered him a hero. As his movies were aired on TV, there was a constant demand for him to "speak," "shake hands," or pose for pictures, and he had infinite patience with the demands. He had an almost human understanding of people's needs and how to anticipate and minister to those needs. As an example, one of my nephews was born with splayed feet; that means they turned out. In order to correct this, the doctor had prescribed braces and told my sister and her husband not to expect the baby to walk at the normal time. One day, quite to everyone's surprise, Bandit was seen walking past the window very slowly with the baby walking as he hung on to Bandit's tail. Bandit was teaching the baby to walk!

Bandit and I got together again at a time in my life when everything that I considered valuable or held dear was gone. It probably was the lowest point in my life. I would take trips out to the beach just to get away from everyone and reflect on where my life was going. The only companion I wanted was Bandit. Although he was a lot older, he still wanted me to throw a ball and play with him. Those trips were my therapy sessions as Bandit gently and playfully coaxed me out of my solitude. Things began to look differently and I began to concentrate on my relationship with the Lord. This led me into areas I'd never been in before, one of which was the detention ministry. Bandit came along as I ministered to the teenage boys. He performed his magic on them, drawing them out of their depression as he had done with me. They all loved to hear his story, especially the part about my finding him in a 'prison.' However, I soon noticed that the demands of being a celebrity were getting to be too much for him so I gradually fazed him out of the prison ministry. He was slowing down and started acting like the old dog he was. I noticed too that he was in pain and was having trouble negotiating steps and climbing into a car by himself.

It just so happened that Christmas was near and I was asking the Lord to help make it a special time. For once I wanted to make Christmas a spiritual, not a commercial, enterprise. Realizing that Bandit was special to me and was fulfilling the need I had to be loved, it was hard for me to imagine my life without him; I would cry just thinking about not having him around. One day while praying, I pictured myself going to the stable at Bethlehem, carrying my old friend in my arms and presenting him to the Infant Jesus, who lay smiling up at me from the manger. I explained to Jesus that my gift was the only thing I had left that I treasured. Slowly and deliberately I placed Bandit beside the Baby Jesus, and with a breaking heart, I turned and walked away. Well my prayer became a reality that Christmas Eve. Arriving home I discovered Bandit out on the lawn unable to stand and in extreme pain. Seeing him in that situation tore my heart apart, and reluctantly and painfully I called the local Animal shelter. Feeling like Abraham of the Old Testament, I tenderly placed Bandit in my car for the last time.

At the animal shelter, the Officer took him very gently from me. Sadly and agonizingly I stood waiting outside until he brought me back Bandit's collar.

"It's all over," said the Officer as he placed Bandit's collar in my hands.

Only by the grace of God was I able to get back in my car and drive away.

All the way home, through my tears I painfully reflected, "Lord, I know he was just an old dog, but he meant the world to me and I loved him. Could you please let me know if he is with You?"

The next day was Christmas, and I was still feeling the loss as I arrived at camp to conduct a Communion service. The boys were at a low point too; they had nothing to give to their families who would be visiting later. Our service was held in a small room and the only decoration was a small Nativity Set on the table/altar. I talked to the boys about the spirit of giving and used the popular song "The Little Drummer Boy" as an example. I explained that people place too much emphasis on expensive gifts when the greatest gift they could give was the thing they placed the least value on - themselves.

I suggested that, while receiving the Eucharist, they prayerfully present themselves to the Infant Jesus and offer Him the one precious gift that no one else could give - themselves.

I explained to them that I already did that some time ago, but that this year I gave the Lord something else that was very precious and dear to me.

Not wishing to tell them about Bandit's having to be put to sleep, and not wanting to break down, I struggled to continue with the service.

When it was over and the boys began to leave, I accidentally leaned over the table and looked inside the manger scene. What a beautiful surprise! There besides the Baby Jesus was a little plastic statue of a dog in the exact spot where I had placed Bandit in my meditation.

For a few seconds I stood there in shock. "It's a dog!" I blurted out.

"No, Mr. Scotty, that's a wolf." said one of the young men standing next to me.

"No," I replied, "it's a dog," as my eyes filled up with tears of joy. "Believe me, it's a dog!"